The Night I Heard Everything

∞

Mary Carroll-Hackett

FUTURECYCLE PRESS
www.futurecycle.org

Library of Congress Control Number: 2015933569

Copyright © 2015 Mary Carroll-Hackett
All Rights Reserved

Published by FutureCycle Press
Lexington, Kentucky, USA

ISBN 978-1-938853-76-0

*for my mother, my children, and John
for teaching me what faith means*

Contents

The Night I Heard Everything...7
One History of Water...8
A Coin, and an Egg...9
She Gave Her Meat and Milk...10
When the Moon is Dry..11
Knots We Tied Ourselves...12
Pregnant Snake Charmer for Hire..13
Dirty Feet...14
The Visible Woman..15
Seven Deadly..16
They Knew She Was a Saint..17
That Hymn You Recall..18
Moses, the Word Means...19
The Girl Who Read the Land...20
Before Newton's Theory of Light...22
Here, Touch Here..23
This City, She Loves Me...24
Hills Like Ceremony...25
And When You Dreamt of Women Drowning..................26
My Friend Who Loves Maps...27
In Louisiana, They Say Not to Plant....................................28
Cambodian Jungle Woman Found.......................................29
Quoting Houdini...30
The Skin Project..31
Mouth Music..32
The Study of Patterns Produced by Vibrating Bodies.............33
What But Skin..34
The Deer in the Dark Said...35
Love Is the Concrete Stair...36
What Hands Do After a Death —..38
The Man Who Maps Crash Sites...39
Being Dead in Carolina..40
Without Her Feet..41

The Maasai Don't Bury Their Dead..42
When I Miss You Most..43
The Cherokee Word for Warm...44
Dark Brown Is My Favorite Shape..45
Eight Rules for Ghosts...46
In the Thin Places..48
Finding the Bear's Bed..49
On the Second Anniversary of Your Death................................50
I Want to Bring the Birds...51
Someday the Woman You Will Be..52
All Things Are Number..54
How to Save the World, and Ourselves.....................................55
Sound Must Have Its Medium..56
Acknowledgments

The Night I Heard Everything

I heard you, in the middle of it all, explaining the relationship
between two specific electrical currents to your ex-wife,
needing her to see the way you see, to feel the transformation
of light into sound, music that makes the shape of your
knowing. I sat on my stoop, hundreds of miles away,
keeping time with trees, and heard oak leaves speak
in a thousand harmonic tongues.

Above, a ballet of bats began their broadband sweep of the
night, echo and duration their tools, measured modulation,
intensity and frequency, pulse and interval, and I recalled how
for all the years I'd known you, you closed your eyes when
music played, your body tuned, how you crooned across my
naked ribs, up and over the crescent curve of my belly.

Science tells the one disadvantage bats face: any echo
returning can only be evaluated for the space of a millisecond,
the fast downward sweep of the song never remaining at any
one frequency for long.

You sang "Good Day Sunshine" and "Cinnamon Girl,"
the music in bed with us, as we turned light and sound into
current, loved skin into composition.

I whispered, to the oaks tumbling with sound around me,
and to you, the you then and the you now: *Listen.*
Then listen again.

One History of Water

involves pilgrims, not the hand-turkey kind, not the brass-buckled blind bulletin board thieves, but travelers, proselytes, seekers, willing to walk over grassy plains, dry for more than thirty years with scant rain, drought forcing out this parade of the thirsty, stumbling due east across the altiplano toward the blue white peaks of the Andes. They chanted pleas for the rumble of thunder, to sweeten potatoes, the meat of alpaca and llama, for fish scorched to leather in the same dusty lake bed where the creator emerged, to shape earth and the people with damp fingers, where the ancestors lingered at the gateway of the sun, where undone shrines crouched on cracked coasts, where the need to persist was even greater than the terror of ghosts. What priest would we seek, I wonder, willing to smash the *kero,* ceremonial cup battered against the skull of a neighbor, who would we place on the altar stone, when the wind cries for decades, clatter of our own bones ever drier and hotter? Every language has a word for water.

A Coin, and an Egg

is what they found, ritual offerings dug into pits and joints
in the floor, a group of small bowls, sewing needles, tiny
instruments, metal sharpened to points, in a room constructed
of ancient ground at Sardis, thousands of years ago, part of
the temple of Artemis, she even older than Greece, she Homer
called Queen of the Wildlands, Mistress of the Animals,
she who also protected the girl-child and heaving woman,
virginity and birth, guardian of all things feminine.

A coin, and an egg, they found within, gifts they left her.

A woman, later, much later, knelt on that same earth,
to brush away time, peel back the millennia now thin as
paper, and there the bowls, still filled with dirt, dissembled
to find within that coin hammered perfectly flat, engraved
with a lion's image, and that egg, perfectly intact, except for
a hole carefully punched in its shell.

This one's special, the woman's Princeton colleagues said,
we can tell.

The woman, Artemis' daughter, brought the egg close to her
face, her breath moving in the space to where dust coated it,
and peered through the hole, carefully, carefully, peered into
the darkness, the shell's interior still, and black.

She said nothing. Just knew the holy will of all women
looking back.

She Gave Her Meat and Milk

to her children, for years, claiming to be a vegetarian, her
portions of each meal steaming on their plates, any extra,
carcass picked clean with her own mother's fingers, pulled
from the bony chicken bought carefully on sale at Food Lion,
the cold white sweetness in their glasses, the brown earthiness
of tough stew beef simmered tender with onion gravy —
they ate what was hers, and they grew. She smiled at the
milk mustaching their little mouths, the clanging music of
forks hitting plates, and ate her own bowl of beans, greens
grown in the garden she kept, rice to fill the same space
beneath her ribs where once these babies — now children,
now adults — had swum. She ate whatever remained,
every bite a prayer they never heard her say.

When the Moon is Dry

and waning, cut rail fence, if you want them to stay straight.
Wait till she's dark to lay shingles and shakes. Set fence posts
in the dark of the moon, too, to prevent them from rotting,
and always set those posts the way the tree grew, root end
down, limbs now phantoms scattered around where you
stand, while the moon looks softly on, as you, hammer and
ax in hand, attempt some vain stay at what can never truly
be held, at what the moon knows is already gone.

Knots We Tied Ourselves

taught as little girls, especially in the sixties, from the French, *macramé*. While our older sisters fought in the trenches, tear-gas and heat, we gathered in basements for Girl Scouts, Brownies — little people, they called us — little women sitting around a table where we knotted and looped, scooped cord up into our hands, our wrists, twisting it all first into bracelets we bound round our thin arms, then keychains, and, eventually, hangers for plants, gifts to be wrapped in tissue and given in spring to our mothers and aunts.

No one ever said, stroking the crowns of our little-girl heads, that these knots we fashioned, so earnest in our little-girl passions, came to us from women held captive, centuries of being taught their womanness was evil, a thing to be hidden — reviled, they failed to tell us — from the Arabic, *miqramah*, a silken prison, an embroidered veil.

Pregnant Snake Charmer for Hire

paid in rubles and shekels, dollars and dimes, each time she
unwinds her song, one hand on her stretched swollen belly,
the other hand, long fingers, splayed like a brooch, like a cage,
like a flower at her throat. Her dark hair in ringlets, falling
over breasts ripe with milk, dances as she sings, her voice her
flute, the call to the python coiled on the ground at her feet.
Meet me, she sings, *rise and meet me,* while the crowd falls to
murmurs and whispers, the snake undulating as it lifts, to her
knees, wrapping himself round her hips, writhing across her
mother's stomach, up between her breasts, slowing, stopping
only when it brushes its bifurcated tongue across her lips.

People swoon, the moon turning her into Serpentina,
the legend, the freak, the python, golden and older than
the fear that holds the crowd still until—*Leave me,* she sings,
go and leave me.

In the off-season, she pays rent from a glass jar on the counter,
rent on the cottage she shares with her man Tim, a carpenter
who builds churches, and she makes mac and cheese, keeps it
warm for him until he gets home. They drink Sprite and watch
TV, and in the middle of the night, Tim stirs, and she quiets
him, pulls him over to her, rests his hand on her belly, so they
both feel the this way and that way curling of the little boy
they'll name Gunnar, after Tim's dad.

In a glass case, at the foot of their bed, Firecracker,
the python, sleeps, glows crayon yellow in the weak white
streetlight coming in through the window, as the night goes
on and on.

Dirty Feet

and dirty fingernails, angels, ten thousand of them, living in
trailers, canned angels, holy meat, languishing in the Carolina
heat, driving up from Kinston, and Shelby, and Bear Grass,
and Calico, driving in the vans they bought secondhand at
Car Coop, headed to the ocean, to Buxton, to Avon, to Duck,
for a day, for a week, seeking some sun and some water.
Wings tucked into tank tops, T-shirts from Walmart,
glittered with sayings like "Hot Stuff," "Daddy's Girl,"
and "Talk to the Hand." They dig angel toes into the hot
sand, and pray over pimento cheese sandwiches, and pickles,
and Tupperware pitchers of tea. On the best days, they run
into the sea, hugging their dirty-faced babies close, then
holding them up to the wide white sky, whispering in ten
thousand languages: *Remember, no matter what they say,
that you can fly.*

The Visible Woman

when she was a child, could make herself invisible, so
wrapped she was in dreams of angels in the trees, and aliens
in the cornfield, and becoming Houdini, tied up in sheets
she shook free from the bed, begging her brother to bind her
hands and feet so she could show him how they would both
escape. She remade herself into Joan of Arc, burning to be free,
or a girl with Tsalagi eyes among the Nunne'hi, those wise
and beautiful spirit people, seen only when they want to be.
Writing backward, right to left, hieroglyphs and letters turned
the world and time into things she could bend, rendered them
malleable, so she traveled back to Snowbird, heard the stories
of the disappearing, found the clearing there in Ireland, that
hill at Tara where the light-eyed ones vanished from this
middle plane. She learned the art of not remaining, invisibility
her best work. After all, being seen meant being hurt. So even
now, in her visible life, she remembers, years away from that
trailer heat and cornfields, filled with fists and flesh and anger,
she knows how not to matter, recalls the disappearing songs
the angels in the pine trees brought her, the magic words—
Now you see her, now you don't—that gypsy-eyed Houdini
taught her.

Seven Deadly

reasons the nuns gave us for lying, and for memorizing the lies in Latin, *SALIGIA* printed on the dusty chalk board: *Superbia, Avaritia, Luxuria, Invidia, Gula, Ira, Acedia* — Sister Carmelita quoting the Book of Proverbs about what the Lord hateth. Dennis plotted a political career, a tiny man already bent on world domination, his freckled hands clutched in prayer and sweating. Dom folded ruled paper into spaceships, and stars, origami of his own making, licking the folds, then tearing it into being what he wanted, what he would take from the heavens. Melody and Lisa, blonde and protestant, sat with their ankles crossed, practicing their pretty cursive, tossing notes back and forth, linking their names in the margins of notebooks to the boy of the week, sweet and sealed into their little-girl hearts. I sat at the edge of the room, stared out the parochially green window, watching the birds on the playground, sparrows fat and red, a sudden jay, the doves hovering in the shade, and hoped — prayed — they'd never know how, even as children, how completely sinful we already were.

They Knew She Was a Saint

because she took great care with her visions, testing testing
so as to ascertain they were not diabolically inspired, fasting
fasting so as to clear her body bone by bone, making room
for God, losing losing flesh alone, choosing to move toward
beatification, blessing the body, saving the body, preserving
the body, vowing the body unto God and God only, stone
floors cold cold against naked thighs, December air cold cold
on bared breasts, eyes lifted, murmuring *remember remember
the rest*, eyes raised praising praising, eyes turned to the
whites, turned toward the sky, turned toward heaven,
giving over, giving in, giving up to spirit only, *surrender*,
surrendering until they found her in her cell, her self-made
cell, naked, skin blue and glowing, blood flowing flowing
the way blood flows, holy and hot and red until it stops,
and they lifted her, lifted her nude blue remains, there for
days and days before they found her and lifted her in their
strong man arms, her weight like air, like nothing, like nothing
at all, but perfect, perfectly preserved, perfectly incorrupt and
incorruptible, and as they witnessed, witnessed and testified
for all the centuries to come, when they found her and lifted
her, her frail flesh, frail body of flesh, body with bones like
birds, like the hollowest of hours, was clouded, surrounded,
floating in, floating on, encompassing them, enshrouding all
of us, in the sweet sweet, heavenly sweet, scent of flowers.

That Hymn You Recall

from childhood days bent into deep Carolina night, the
hymn your sister used to sing the dark away, never had all
the words you needed *last night I dreamed* seeded doubt turned
you feverish and frantic, burning you out of sweated sheets
I saw a man your bare feet skittering on linoleum, trailer floor
humming, you running for the hard-packed sand there in the
yard, running *he called my name* out to where the leafless trees
spiked fields of feed corn and tobacco *he took my hand* hiking
rows and rows of not-knowing, not knowing if the creator
he bade me look could actually be sung to, could hear the song,
the other way rising up from a long broke world, whether the
creator would pay any mind, *'twas then I heard* no matter how
much you sang, or whether the creator, just like the bosses
and teachers and government workers who came with their
clipboards and scuffed shoes *my savior say* had actually really
just given up on this place.

Moses, the Word Means

"son of" in Egyptian, see Ramses, Ra-moses, son of Ra;
means "to be born of," *mes* or *mesu*. See Thut-moses, not Tut,
our slack way of calling that son of Thoth, god of moon,
magic and writing, who overcame the curse of Ra and helped
Isis get her groove back. And in Galilee, see Jesus; not Jesus —
yeah, his mother called him Eashoa, across the yard and
through the gate, her son always late for supper *Eashoa!*
Come eat! in Aramaic, never Greek. In years to come, his boys,
all Hebrew-tongued, might have said *Oh Yeshua,* "oh yeah
it's you" from the root *yod-shin — ayin,* "to deliver, to save,
to rescue," inscribed into incantation prayer bowls near
where the stone was rolled away, but not the twice-removed
from Ellinika *Iesous* (ee yeh sooce), never appearing in
scripture, but twisted into gospel anyway, sanctified —
justified! — justifying, rationalizing all *in the name of,*
not knowing even that we don't know, don't care,
what we say.

The Girl Who Read the Land

lived in a trailer, not a vine-covered cottage as the story might have gone, but a single-wide with water stains and thrift store chairs on red-dirt land in Carolina. She shoved baby-girl hands, fat and dimpled, against the roll-out windows into the air, and ate tomato soup from a can with her daddy, and took violet walks with her mama, running through the cemetery at the Primitive Baptist, calling the names of the dead carved into crooked gray stones, names and names and names that she wasn't old enough yet to read, that she shouldn't have known. *Tell me what you see, baby,* her mama would say, her mama all pretty and fine-boned with little doll-feet who taught the girl to walk barefoot and dance the jitterbug and walk between rows of cotton and tobacco and beans, who gave the little girl crackers and juice in salad dressing cruets for saying Mass in a kitchen chair, words in Latin in her little-girl mouth wrapped in her Southern tongue as if they'd always been there, while her mama, sitting at the tiny trailer table, with her coffee cup and glasses, said soft in the after-dinner air, *Tell me what you hear, baby.* What she saw and what she heard were people made of light, shiny as the Casper cartoons she giggled at over Cheerios with her brother, but who weren't in the TV but in the corner, and sitting on the scratchy settee, and out in the sand pile her mama had made by hauling sand in trash bags from the lake, and in church on their knees when her uncle the priest said Mass on Sunday, and who weren't always white, sometimes gold and sometimes purple, and sometimes every color all at once like the prisms her daddy had brought her as a present, and hung in the window, saying *Look at all you can see, baby.* What she could see rose from the land, like heat waves, transparencies, movies, just for her. Her mama said,

What the land remembers, that's what you see, baby. So the transparencies were memories: dark-skinned dancers with their long-lidded eyes, the men's chests streaked with red and yellow paint, the women's hair heavy like silk falling over their shoulders, mamas clutching their babies, warriors with tears and blood on their faces, pretty brown children with kinky hair, black women with skin slick and shining and greasy with field heat, little white girls in bonnets and aprons and starving in lost places, feet blue and bleeding, in the Croatan woods on the way to the beach, bearded white men, lost too, but later in blue and in gray, torn and ragged and dirty, walking, walking, marching, on the same road, the same way, no matter how many times the girl looked down and then back, day after day. When she got older, she closed her eyes, to the pictures, to the sounds, and rested her head against the nubby seat of the station wagon. When she got older, she called it the loop, the seeing, the call and didn't question at all why sometimes she would just suddenly cry in a new place, the ground breaking like hearts beneath her feet and time dissolving like rain, filled with face after face, lined with pain and wanting. She opened her eyes and gave them all she had in answer to those centuries of longing, looking directly into their hurt, spirits so broken and tender, and again and again and again saying, *I see you, I see you, and I will remember.*

Before Newton's Theory of Light

his mother said he came too soon, in the same year Galileo
died, born small enough to fit in a quart mug, crooning,
curled up at her side, left to sleep and dream of alchemy and
space and time. Did he first see them then, those corpuscles
of color streaming before his infant eyes, gnawing his rosebud
fist as he recognized reflection and finite velocity, kinetic
energy streaming? Or was that later when, at seventeen,
he failed at farming, too bent on the hidden Biblical messages
that called him to the back of the barn—hiding to learn
Hebrew, fixated on the Book of Daniel—again and again,
a million words of notes, isolating the day of crucifixion,
predicting the Jews' return to Israel and that year, not long
from now, he said the world would end? Did he ponder
material point and force in those taverns where he hunted
counterfeiters, pockets turned with faulty coin? Or was he
even then doing God's work, setting us in motion toward the
realization of illusion, showing us the limitations of our range,
made as we are of material points—the only representative
of reality, its—our—only truth being that all is subject
to change?

Here, Touch Here

just beneath the ribs you kissed when you were nearly twenty-three and I was a girl knee-deep in meadow, fescue, timothy, mustard, the wild ginger I had just learned from my grandmother a few weeks before we met. Dancing in that bar, that night, I wanted to tell you how to spot wild ginger, how Carolina, where we both grew, banned spreading cornflower seeds, and I most wanted to tell that you smelled of sweet clover, and sun. In my silence, I named you *shining one*. Later, while you slept, I whispered secrets into your hair — how black snakeroot would keep you strong, rue and thistle protect you, how the plant I named as spikenard — lavender — would lead you in my direction, when our time came. In the morning, I left rosemary behind that you might, just might, remember. Because as false at times as desire may seem, it isn't. Nor is the humid wish for love, steaming, sweating, our second skins, those made of glass, the ones we fear the most will shatter.

(for D)

This City, She Loves Me

like twelve-bar blues, uneven eights liquifying asphalt
beneath my wheels, inside my shoes, till I'm all but coming
undone in the turnaround, on my knees, unbound, looking
up from the street, store awnings droop sweat-sexy shoulders
in low-country heat. Sing to me, baby, delta growl, shuffle
slow, slash and slide — the city glides me till I'm straight-up
hollow-bodied, held tight, cotton-necked, swollen — and the
good kinda wrecked only comes from being thoroughly,
shamelessly, wantonly loved.

Hills Like Ceremony

rising where he's never seen them before, and he thinks perhaps, through her, he could learn abandon, to quit worrying, to just feel. Maybe then he could sleep — finally — his body in release, slowly drifting, one hand hanging loose between her knees, bodies sharing half a century between them. Maybe she can show him that longing doesn't have to hurt, that their Now can make a space for joy, and possibility remains, still golden and sweet. Half asleep, she rubs her lips against his stubbled cheek, cat-like tongue catching the corner of his mouth as she whispers to the curly-haired boy he used to be: *I'll show you – if you let me – how music tastes like amber, how skin can shift like sand, touch can have a taste, and everything you've ever thought you couldn't have but want so much is right here, just within reach of your hand.*

And When You Dreamt of Women Drowning

did you see their bowed arms like stems rising from green
garden foam and salt and the white of bone? Even their names
unravel in the pulling fingers of the tide. *Listen. Look.* I hide
those women beneath my breasts, sisters salty and just a little
rough. I ride their backs when you ride mine, your fingers
dimpling my hips, my spine a swinging bridge to all women
who know the power of giving ourselves away.

There, just there, where all of history crosses into being,
in that patch of memory made rough, what every man's hands
understand: longing bone white and whistling — that touch
you dream when you shift, when you toss in tangled sheets,
most alone.

My Friend Who Loves Maps

traces what's possible with the fine tip of her finger.
I like getting lost, she says, the map wider than dreams,
seamed with blue lines and red highways. Her eyes linger,
looking for all the places she hasn't seen yet, folding the South
Pole into a history of Pittsburgh steel. *Listen,* she says, and in
the low rumble of her voice, wet velvet streets glisten beneath
tires, deepening the rip of Harley wheels across memory.
Just think what they give you, she says, *feel it,* and I am flooded
with intersections where rivers drum mountains to stone,
the mystery moves of men's fingers where soft thigh meets
hip, where the history of canyon and roadway call to bone,
dare you to make that the low lean into the wind, rounding
that curve and the next, so far from home, so far from
being alone.

(for Jan Beatty)

In Louisiana, They Say Not to Plant

on Good Friday, that blood will run from the cold
ground, but Miss Pearl, my mountain grandmother,
believed otherwise, believed that any seed planted that
day would thrive. Her gnarled fingers clawed at the clay
outside the cinderblock house she and Pap built in their
sixties, the block painted as pale green as the peas she set to
climb on sticks, on poles, on whatever she scruffed up into
the garden. Peas and potatoes dug into that hillside in Nebo,
and later, when it warmed, tomatoes and okra, some soft-
faced petunias, touching their velvet bodies with her cotton-
picking scarred hands. But not beans—she planted no more
beans after that winter my mama was twelve and Pap had
run off and not come back for that long cold time, leaving
her with a tribe of children to feed on nothing but the beans
she'd scratched from the garden the summer before and
canned, stacked on shelves, on the floor, jar after jar green
in the weak light from the window.

Years later, in the slow places all lives go, in the soft twilight
of her dementia, where no matter what he'd done or that
he was gone, she still hunted for Pap—this time between
the night hallways and the doors my mama locked to keep her
safe from wandering. In those waning days without calendars
to consult, without schedules to turn to, she still knew it was
Good Friday, still scrambled from her bed, still called for my
mama to *Come on git to the garden* where there were seeds to
planted, needs to be tended, souls to be fed.

Cambodian Jungle Woman Found

brought back, given a hero's return, until without the words
to tell why, she fled, hid to monkey-cry in an outdoor toilet.
Lost as a child, out herding buffalo eighteen years ago, then
gone, disappeared into the shade of the Kapok and Durian
trees, from girl to woman, eating the sweet pink swirl of
jambu fruit snatched from leather leaves, strangler figs shared
with the gibbons and bats; sleeping curled like a cat beneath
a mangrove moon. Now, that civilized nonsense of clothes,
and soup bowls and spoons, and combing her hair, was
simply more than she could bear. So she starved, crawled
rather than walked, ripped out the IV needles they carved
into her thin arms, these people with their talk, all that noise
like tin rattling, like traffic, like the havoc of the village they'd
brought her to, all bleat and bellow from their mouths and
hard shoes on wood floors, yelling at each other, this woman
who kept saying *moth-er* over and over, this man who held her
arm so tight, the children gaping from the door, their teeth so
white and sharp, she felt them bite into bone, even from across
the room, even as she cried, even as they sang together,
those hairless children, some sound again and again—
welcomehomewelcomehome.

Quoting Houdini

can be dangerous if done in bars or on trains these days —
My brain is the key that sets me free — anywhere in plain sight,
when escape, even the notion of escape, is as punishable as
running drugs and political defining of fear — listen here! no
one escapes — no shades of gray anymore, that magical back
hatch, secret door in the painted box — go ahead and check
the locks — *No performer should attempt to bite off red-hot iron
unless he has a good set of teeth* — then spin, two times, three —
secrets you away into custody, you person of interest you.
*Fire has always been, and seemingly will always remain, the most
terrible of the elements,* terror burned into us, turned back on us,
igniting obedience. You can be made to disappear — *I'm tired
of fighting, Dash. I guess this thing is going to get me* — poof —
see? Gone, one by one, illusions and constitution all undone.
Houdini said *the chief task is to overcome fear,* bound and
chained under water without relief — *What the eyes see
and the ears hear, the mind believes* — who was Erik Weiscz
anyway? Look there, beside you on the metro, hands in his
lap, or go find him at the corner huddling into his fatigues
and knit cap, the woman with the briefcase, or the baby,
on her hip, worry at her lips, her eyes on you as if she sees
you naked and tied up behind the glass, waiting to cross the
street, as you pass, she mouths the words: *answer – tell – pray,
answer – look – tell – answer, answer – tell.*

The Skin Project

involves yours, and mine, lined and curved and carrying all
that we have managed to survive, fifty lifetimes in fold and
lip, teeth like tines against hip, lavender ankle, tangle of feet,
no longer choosing, simply following my finger to trace the
line of your cheek, your hand losing its path, bent knee, the
laughter of thighs, the sigh of my belly. You whisper into my
ribs, wait for the echo, I know what you want me to speak—
*This, this is the way. Put your head on my chest and listen to what
my heart says.* We both know bones to be brighter in winter,
lips and kiss an entirety, words we couldn't know when we
were young pass forth to tongue, go toward—not back—
this ancient act, this searching for forms of fire.

Mouth Music

puirt-a-beul — like the old Scots did it, this rhythm of throat and tongue and lung and heart — never ever forget the heart — more than just singing, this ringing of nonsense words, in a place where the sound is what matters — the instrument is the heart — never ever forget the heart — those vocables, those sound effects, no instruments needed for the mouth tunes to feed even the poorest souls — for even the poor have hearts — never ever forget the heart — spending years to learn the proper breathing, especially the sounds needed for dancing, words chosen to please the feet — and release the prayer of the heart — dance is prayer for the heart — songs to ease the hurting, the dog-long days of working — the call and response of the heart — never ever forget the heart — go cantering, fiddle and *diddlage,* 'cause music is where it starts — chamber to chamber, the heart — always remember the heart.

(for Kopana Terry)

The Study of Patterns Produced by Vibrating Bodies

*Of letters I am a. Of compounds I am the dual.
I alone am unending time.* —Bhagavad Gita 10.33

The science of sound did not begin with Galileo, no matter
how I love him, but farther back, scientist Hans Jenny found,
what the old ones always knew — that all is made of light
and sound, regardless of how we try to ground ourselves.
That shy Swiss man, with his crystal tonoscope and search for
wave phenomena, quartz sand spread round on black drum
plates, carefully poised to oscillate, set into motion by singing
focused through a cardboard tube, produced Chladni patterns,
low tones creating simple forms, higher tones more complex,
the sand shivering into hexagons and spirals, a webbed and
lacy display of sound in ordered form, the song, the dance
of matter.

Older still, the vowels he spoke, spilling ancient tongues —
Sanskrit, Hebrew — through the tube, spun the sand into
their own true shapes, into something far past symbols,
this singing then of sacred texts, no mirror this, but concrete
transformation of physical reality — the *a,* the *u,* the long *ee*
sound of *i* — the art of *making* in the tender kiss of frequency
and amplitude, vibrating into sight all that we believe exists,
all we think we know. So speak it. Make it so.

What But Skin

can open into flowers, blossom at a touch, rooted in bone, fine-lined topographical map of a life? Yours smelled of cinnamon and sage, and sweat, and smoke, fires you built to hold back the cold on those lonely Georgia nights, flames you coaxed into being as solace, as inquiry, as prayer.

You said, *I've been singing to you my whole life.*

In those same woods where you'd brought me, you unwrapped a lifetime of loneliness, like a test, then watched my face, waiting to see if I would reject you.

I fingered the scar at the corner of your mouth, left there years before by an unkind hand. You kissed my palm, your mouth lingering open on my skin. We began again, in a stand of Georgia pine, creating new rituals, our own gestures of survival and surrender, shelter against a world we had not known, either of us, to be tender.

The Deer in the Dark Said

be gentle with him, in the quick click and flutter of her
velvet ears, too large like wings, caught in the light of a
whole moon, in the young geometry of her face. There, in that
nighttime place beneath the oak, just outside my open door,
her dancer's feet singing, skittering acorns across the frozen
dirt, she laughed, and ducked her head, saying, as the old
women tell it — we offer ourselves, go willingly to the killing,
to be had, that is our medicine, our lot. But it is not. No species
long survives who relents, who gives themselves to hunters,
clawed or fanged or drunken orange-clad. Fleet limbs for
broken field sprints, hooves honed sharp against the bark
of wolves and short-faced bears and mountain lions, and
now even the cougar there takes our sick and old ones first.
A healthy buck, a wary doe, can take an eye, break a mouthful
of teeth. Anyone who lives wounded knows what we mean,
what survival is bequeathed to us.

So give the frankness of your wonder, your child's eyes,
a thankful day. That is the way. See, she said, even in your
light now, that buck there flare-lit, overexposed, and yet he
stands, his head turned, well-fed and strong, he burns, shows
no ribs, no fear, even though the hardest thing sometimes is
just to live. Give him what's tender. Remember he still wears
the spotted shirt, under his long man's bones, the roar and
tumbled fear of shadow and stone crowding his path, even as
he gazes straight at you, daring you to come here, come closer,
daring you to make this last.

Love Is the Concrete Stair

there behind your Nanny's house, where her woman-name was Mildred and she so loved your granddaddy, her Jake, her handsome Jake with his Cherokee eyes and big hands who always called her Mildred, not Jackie, not the nickname she was given as a kid, short for *jackass,* but my Mildred, my love, her Jake with his gentle mouth twisting just a little as she taught his big hands to crochet in their tender years of going, together in the tender years after he quit building churches, and settled in between cornbread and crochet needle so small in his hand and kisses on the head from his Mildred, from the woman he had cherished forever. Love is the aluminum awning, weathered to gray, there behind that little clapboard house where the cardinal skittered like tattered red paper, driving Smoky the gray-as-the-awning cat crazy enough that he jumped off the roof of the aluminum carport, echoing all the way to the hard ground below, and woke us up from a just-loved sleep in the same room where Jake had loved Mildred and Mildred so, so loved him back. Love is the pocket in the blue lumpy bathrobe so big, too big, that you loved so much, the pocket where you kept butterscotch and Andes candies that you brought out to me as a surprise, while I had my coffee and smoke and tried to find language, me and the cardinal not yet in our songs, the pocket where you rested your hand, your guitar player's hand, your photographer's hand, the hand that loved me, the backs of my knees and my hollowed neck, the way Jake loved Mildred out there with the camellias, the pocket you fiddled in, laughing, saying *Call me when you got words, girl,* before disappearing back under the awning into the house to wait for me, before disappearing for good, before dying, before dying, before dying, and leaving me there, on the concrete stair.

Smoky the cat ran off. But the cardinal still scratches seed
from the burnt yellow grass, its wings the only color,
right now, that I can see, or that matters.

What Hands Do After a Death —

they forget. Her hands didn't know anymore. Nothing other
than the bean pods, planted outside the door, the leathery
switch and hang of shell and seed, her hands didn't know
themselves, knew only the snap and swing of vining things,
beans like leather britches, sewn together and hung like the
old women had shown her. Her hands had always known,
as had her feet, the fold of towels, the path back home,
the perfect curve of cursive vowels the nuns demanded,
the subtle stitch of crewel and needle pulled, the three-strand
braid — all now unsprung. Now her hands dropped and
wrung and slapped and stung, the drinking glass shattered
to shards on hard cold tile, the thread in knots, ink shot across
the page in hieroglyphs, ancient outlines of hurt. Only dirt
made sense, the growth and give, then decay, of seeds,
her hands needing to dig, until a proper hole was made
so that something, anything, might live.

The Man Who Maps Crash Sites

makes handwritten notes in black ink — only black, so as not to be confused with the blue of the rivers, the red elevations — notations on thin paper, one inch equaling one mile, the distance from knuckle to rounded thumb, more or less, legend blurred and creased by the stress of folding and unfolding and refolding, seeking the most direct route, a series of turns done and undone, corrected right, right, finally left, there — on that mountain ridge, near the marshy woods, by that lake where the great herons gather — he finds tangle of metal and foliage and stone, charred, twisted and greasy with smoke, he finds what's left, those things others can't see, the wreckage and how much it matters.

Being Dead in Carolina

means pine sap and stones in red clay, unless you're down
east, then it's pine sap and sand and cypress. It means pockets
of shade in hundred-plus months, humidity that stands like
walls, solid enough we part the curtains of heat with our
hands as we walk across century-turned fields, clods of dirt
held together by memories of tobacco and peanuts, soybeans
and cotton, to a clump of oaks left standing for a hundred-plus
years, untouched in the center of wide hot nothing, oak and
loblolly monuments, in a place where no one and nothing is
forgotten. Someone standing there pulls at a hot stiff collar,
while the preacher recites the Twenty-Third, someone is
named Junior, and someone else will keep the pictures
on a shelf or in a box, dragged out at Christmas along with
sweet potatoes and pecan pie, and while fat babies dangle
from hips, and men gather outside to talk basketball and
fried turkey and politicians—can't trust none of 'em—
the women will lean over the photos, some of them sepia
and bent, tape yellowed at the corners, and they will once
again be mourners, speaking your name out loud, Aunt This,
Uncle That, *Now whose daddy was he again?* And they will
reclaim the lines, reweave themselves into your time,
together and alone, wisdom born of survival heavy
as stone, the nobility of persisting, understanding that
your story is also their own.

Without Her Feet

they found her, buried in an Iron Age grave, this Iron Age
woman, without her feet, just down the hill from the Manor
House Bed & Breakfast, where today Marney O'Connell
makes beds and cinnamon scones for the guests who come
in from the city, winding A350, a short drive down the trunk
road, for a weekend away from what's hard, from what works
them. This woman, barely in her thirties, interred just a stone's
throw from The Cider House Tourist Shoppe, where Marney's
brother Tom who quit the water company job sells miniatures
and paperbacks and maps to the countryside, quilted with
16th-century farmhouses, roll of field, carefully quaint, a
quaint and quiet trip back for those same travelers who want
to pretend, for a day, a gentler way, a kinder time. Tom sells
them maps that they follow in their shiny new boots, bought
for the country, bought for holiday, bought to take them back,
but not so far back, that they know, or even wonder, about the
woman, the Iron Age woman, who was, at some point 3,000
years ago, held down by hands that meant her harm, held
down in the Wiltshire dirt, while they sawed off her feet, and
buried first her, then her feet three meters away, as if to bind
her to that place for all time, buried there, unable to walk,
to run, to ever even dream of escape.

The Maasai Don't Bury Their Dead

declaring the ground too sacred, fearing the bodies will
contaminate the soil, and so they slather them, their mothers
and uncles and sons and daughters in ox fat, great smears to
draw in the scavengers, the white-backed vultures, the ripping
jaws of hyena and jackal, leaving them to the pull and tear of
teeth and beak, beneath the haze and slow white burn of the
African sun, baking, taking body back to brush and sand and
stone. Unless the man dead—and it is always a man—is a
chief, ranked and honored by his tribe, then a shallow grave is
dug, somewhere near a wild fig tree, and the chief's bones and
flesh flung in, an offering to that holy ground, tribute to Enkai,
neither male nor female, both black and red, both benevolent
and angry, no single entity, but god in every aspect, the all in
everything, the everything in all, tree and sky and river and
the rare, rare rain. The laiboni sing songs about the origin of
death, how one man, that first warrior, was given the key to
eternal life but reversed the words, securing death as a natural
fact for us all. Then the desert calls, and they pack and move
on, speaking sweetly of their family gone, referring to them
as *etalaki*—missing—or as *ipa, sampa*—sleeping, especially
the old ones, sleeping for all time, never as dead, or gone.
They move on, and on, knowing the dead remain close and
unseen, beneath each heated foot crossing and recrossing
the vast desert plains, ancestor songs in each precious
and trickling stream.

When I Miss You Most

I wear your clothes, sleep pants and shirts, too big,
enfolding me, hems I step on, sleeves I have to roll up,
pockets deep enough for guitar picks and vegetable seeds,
deep enough for two hands, one to reach out, reach for
again and again, one to reach back and clasp my fingers,
a stroke to say, *Right here, I'm right here, never far away,
I'm right here, where love lingers.*

The Cherokee Word for Warm

also means South, like 75 runs down through Georgia, picked up in Macon in five o'clock traffic, opening faster on the other side, me and this red car and the sun, running the slide home, toward you. After so many years of wandering lost in my own flesh, I prayed for you. *You get what you ask for, girl.* Finally, I came to rest, saw myself unbroken, in that Southern drawl, the way it was meant to be spoken, warm finally, in the drape of bodies, like landscape, or like something even simpler, like music. Outside the streaming window, this land that is you shifts from a ceremony of hills to the open lope of grasses and rivers with wide mouths. Since you walked on, since I'm no longer in a hurry, I stop now, tangle my way through the fields near Perry, outside Cordele. Out there, off the road, in the whorl of sawgrass and Georgia pine and brush, you still say, *Welcome to my country, girl.* And I pray for you again, this time among a prophecy of cabins, a falter of chimneys out in the used-to-be's, like yesterday's altars, burnt and forgiving, stone still warm to the touch.

Dark Brown Is My Favorite Shape

the shape of you and burns like eyes burn black desire like no turning back like skin giving in the color of coffee and creaming into me into you into the pillow turned to the cold side like hiding my face in your back to sleep and to keep from admitting you're leaving bound to leave to die the shape of the lie I tell that you'll live the shape I give belief the shape of you being missed the taste of you permanent the press of your kiss the shape of how it went when you went away the bed bent into the shape of bodies your body the body you left behind mattress outlined into the shape that I take when I lie there thinking I'll drown thinking I might like to drown if it will get me to you back around to what I know is true dark brown like eyes looking back looking back always the shape forever takes the shape of you always the shape of not-gone always the only shape left to hang on to.

Eight Rules for Ghosts

They'll expect you at night, or at least at twilight. They don't understand that you remember, and long for the heat of the sun, especially as it warms a field of bluebells.

Tell them secrets, or make them believe you will; tell them tales of what is to come, or what might, or something to allay (or worsen) what frightens them, what makes them run from the moment at hand. They don't really want to understand, not the hard parts, the truth, but rather just want hearts that race, some momentary proof of their own courage.

Remember location. They'll look for you under bridges, in dark houses and corners, any place where the songs of mourners linger. Put out a sign, so they'll find you.

Don't be too vivid. Choose white or gray, or the tinted color transparency of the old movies they love, and make truths of, or sepia. Sepia is especially acceptable around battlefields and historical zones. Whatever the hue, never shine too brightly. They need to be brighter than you.

Oh, and catch them alone, or in pairs, never anywhere there's a crowd, and be ready to quickly duck out, if the audience grows. Remember, secrets are only treasures to the few who are allowed to know.

When in doubt, howl, or shout, even shriek. Speak in whispers through vents, or a small moan in the hall. Call their names, but just once, so they'll turn around to see, to reach for the sound.

They'll reach for you, too, so don't travel. Stay close, near places and people you know, the people most likely to need you, to feed both your spirits, the ones who will hear it when you sing that old song you both loved. Keep it familiar.

And if all else fails, brush a cheek, a shoulder, with a finger, or a kiss. This, after all, is what lasts the longest, tantalizes the most, the ghost of love when it lingers. When all else fails, give them what they most seek. Make them shiver.

In the Thin Places

I am an immediate supplicant, kneeling in the soft dirt
hollows already there, leaning, reading, not ley lines or
trade routes but, today, in this place, on this land, there is this
man aching, who last century dropped his mud boots by that
yellow door, taking his chair, waiting in tabled silence every
day for the wife to be the wife once more, for the woman to
love him back. His helplessness pulls at my ribs, like weight,
like dark, fills the hollows around my heart, makes my throat
thick, constricted with the words he can't say. I swallow his
sorrow, wrap my arms round my chest, fighting to stand,
in the waves of this man's deep loneliness.

I feel her too, that woman he lives with, the sorrow she
plants like bean rows, things that grow all she can care about,
in place of the babies that didn't come, or half-came, nothing
more than gray shrimp the size of her thumb washed up in
a tumble of bedsheets and blood. She's stowed any joy away
for good, like winter blankets in a chest, and he calls her name
but she sweeps at the steps as if he's not there, willing the
stillness until he gives up, again, and walks out into the dark.

They've made a braid of broken hearts, his, hers, and
now mine, where, if for only this moment, I host their pain,
in this shared space, where heartbreak, like love, lives
outside of time.

Finding the Bear's Bed

the fern they call the bear's bed, Polystichum braunii,
ya na utse sta, takes patience, time. Look in some shaded spot.
Linger near a slope that faces north or east, near water, the line
of shadowed places ferns choose first, then listen, till she sings.
Look for her curled fingers, rising from the central crown,
downward reach, like the old woman's hands, back there,
waiting for you, believing you can bring her relief. Count them
as you walk, the plants, talking softly, and listen—listen!—the
mother bear will speak to you. *Come here,* she'll say, *I'm here.*
Ask her permission, her counsel. Tell her of the woman
waiting for you, back there in knots of pain. Tell her of the
woman's sons, the boys she fed, led with her own hands out of
the caverns of her body, of the blankets she made, shoes, shirts
she sewed and they outgrew long before her needle slowed.
Tell this queen, this curling green, of the neighbors, too, the
other sons and daughters, brothers and sisters, that this old
woman tended, wounds she mended, pots she filled with meat
and beans and herbs, words she sang in praise and with gentle
touch, tell her how much now those same hands betray her.
Ya na utse sta knows. She will show you, then, the medicine
she holds, offering up her own young, their leaf and seal.
There, in the loving green of the Bear's Bed, she will sacrifice
herself so that you and the old mother may heal.

On the Second Anniversary of Your Death

I dreamt a beautiful circle of women, of all ages, speaking in
languages we all understood. We gathered in a good kitchen,
a large room equipped for a mixture of old and new ways of
cooking, beautiful in its possibility. We told of our travels to
this place while we worked together making stew, venison
simmered to a deep dark burgundy, studded with pearls
of garlic and onion, fragrant with oregano, and pepper,
and cinnamon. We snapped beans, and scrubbed carrots,
chopped greens, cubed pumpkin and squash; we sliced
tomatoes, the sweet red juice braceleting our wrists.
My grandmother made bread, the air warm and rich with
the mingling scent of yeast and sugar: loaf bread and fry
bread and biscuits and ribbons of cruller dripping with honey.
Your Great-Aunt Pearl moved behind us, peering over our
shoulders, as she carried in baskets filled with potatoes like
jewels, in colors—purple and sage green, violet red and blues
—I'd never seen. I kept watching the hands, gorgeous with
age, lined and veined with working and mothering and loving
and living, gently lead young smooth fingers to the quick snap
of a pole bean, the deft dance of knife and spoon, the proper
feel of yeast and air and push and pull—not too soon!—
to make the dough rise. Women's knowing filled the room,
soft thrum of voices lifting and falling. My mama called my
name, stepped to where I stirred, saying, *Never alone, girl,
no one who cooks ever cooks alone.* Outside the window, we
knew they were waiting, all those in need gathered 'round,
young and old, those we would feed. Outside, I could hear
you singing, and I swayed to the sound, ladling stew into
stoneware bowls, moving toward the sound, toward service,
toward the always—always and forever—of us.

I Want to Bring the Birds

inside, hold them in my hands, tuck them beneath my shirt, claws and all, feel the sharp tic of each beak, gentle them with my fingers, cradle them against the cage of my ribs, whisper *shh shh shh*—until they each find and linger in their place: the titmice tatting nests into my hair, crested sparrows and juncos perched and singing from my feet, the jays who see me as so much meat, supplier of suet and otherwise foolish and useless, each take a shoulder, their alarm squawk sudden and hard as a couple of crows stand sentry on my back. The chickadees, those flying golf balls with their punk rock eyes and ebony mohawks, bossy and brazen, take my ears, letting me know just how they see this whole thing going, while the shy nuthatch hides, its cinnamon shadow disappearing into my clothes as it hops up my ribs and nuzzles like a newborn near my heart. A pair of doves, and then another, their wings ash-gray and spotted with apricot, nestle on the soft give of my belly; I touch them with just the tips of my fingers, hoping, praying, they'll teach me the tender songs only possible in the dark. One by one, they all settle in, on my limbs, my skin, feathering, resting, and so do I, settle for real, for the first time in years, as I hear and feel their heartbeats steady, slow, and ease finally into a companion rhythm with my own. Or mine to theirs? In my dreams, it doesn't matter. In my dreams, we are the same.

Someday the Woman You Will Be

will knock at your door, and you will put down the book
or broom or glass of tea or cat that you are stroking or using
or drinking or reading, and you will cross the floor in your
striped socks, or in your bare feet, or in the new brown boots
you're wearing to break in, and you'll reach for the door
handle in some absent-minded way, thinking that it's a
salesman, or a witness to the word, or that woman next
door who borrows the oddest things—a cup of shampoo
instead of sugar, vacuum cleaner bags, a snow globe from
New Hampshire she wants to take a photo of—but it won't
be that woman, or witness, or salesman. It will be you.
The well-worn you. The wiser you. The you who knows
you better than you'll ever know yourself in that moment
at the door. She'll have a train ticket, or airfare, or a recipe
for the very muffins you crave most from your childhood,
that little you who remembers the muffins like joy-taste,
like love-feels-like this. Or she'll have nothing at all in
her hands, but all of the knowing you need in her eyes,
and you'll think you recognize her, think you know her,
but you'll be embarrassed to say because you think you can't
remember, and you'll search your memories, trying so hard
to recall, who she is, how you know her, maybe from work,
maybe from some friend of a friend, maybe from hours
spent in bookstores or coffee shops or waiting on corners
for streetlights to change, or maybe she just has one of those
faces. You've been told you have one of those kinds of faces—
the kind you remember even though you never actually know
them—from reflections in shop windows or strangers on a
train. Together, at your door, the two of you, the two yous,
will stand, on that morning, in that cold sunlight, a morning
that maybe you think you have nothing to give, nothing to

offer the day or the world or yourself, and she will know
that fear in your polite but apologetic smile, in the lowering
of your head, in the uncomfortable way you look past her,
over her shoulder, to the house across the street where the
plain-faced husband hauls trashcans to the curb, or to the
maple now burning peach and orange and red in the bite
of autumn air, and you'll try not to, but you'll think about
endings, of marriages, of jobs, of people even, the endings
of lives, and that's when she—the you who has survived
all those endings—she'll straighten the collar of her coat,
or clear her throat, or reach out one gloved hand—no, it will
be bare, her hand, when she reaches out to touch you, your
wrist, bare too at the cuff of your pajama shirt, or dress shirt,
or robe, she'll touch you with her fingers, your fingers, so she
can feel you, and you can feel her, and you do, feel her, feel
you, again—and you'll know she's standing there, on your
stoop, having knocked, having pulled you, for just a moment,
away from the book or the broom or the glass of tea or the cat,
so that you'll know that you are always each moment of every
age, always the child, the adult and the elder, all the yous, and
that, there, in the sharp unsullied light that is the real you,
there are, in fact, no endings, no endings after all.

All Things Are Number

Pythagoras said, honoring those ancestors the negatives —
how can you have less than nothing? — square root of nil,
filled and emptied, standing to be counted everything
we hold to be real — eggs, shoes, number of children born
and buried, clicking praying days and beads and pony-
spotted beans away, minutes carried into lingering hours
of skin, ten fingers to kiss and kiss again, no measurable
inch missed — that spinning out of all that is, language
Galileo gave to God, that gives us the songs we sing alone,
fingers plucking string into sound, clinking down coins —
seven in all — partitioning paradise into levels, at last for
some of us. But poor Pythagoras, dumbfounded at the
thought, underestimated the magic — so far beyond what
reason limits — missed the unending shades of what we can
imagine, these prime and primal minds of ours, in natural
states, already uncountable, as infinite as heaven's gates.

How to Save the World, and Ourselves

When the name of a place is a bird, when the bird is a song,
when the song is a prayer, when the prayer is a footstep, when
the footstep is a drum, when the drum is a womb thundering
open, giving birth to a sky so wide that even the stars chase
across it, falling, calling out to each other, we can save it,
we can, if we just remember.

Sound Must Have Its Medium

like Shakti to Shiva, existence to energy, the static only known
in the undulating dynamic.
Sound into being—

From the Middle French, *compression,* from the Latin,
compressionem, pressing, coming, together, a noun of action,
being *rarefied,* less dense, spreading and surrendering, pushing
and pulling. Sound waves moving through matter—liquid,
solid, gas—like mystery—

like all those worlds born of nothing, into something, into all
that we think we know:

Creation stories unfold: the Lowa, the Uncreated, alone in
water in ancient times, humming the Marshall Islands into
rising, plants and animals sung into soil, lips at sea level
delighted at his own song...*run run run drum drum drum*

The duet of Tawa and the Spider Woman—creation told
in Micronesia—the Tirawa—space itself

sounding itself into every aspect imaginable, every part of
the whole. In the land of the Seal People, a long-legged hare
stretched muscle and tendon across the dark that was all
and whispered that word—
day.

And you.

Even now, can you hear me?
Your voice is still the only thing making me real.

Acknowledgments

Some of the poems here were originally published in the following journals. Thanks to these editors for their encouragement and for their continuing efforts toward the beautiful work, the good and too often thankless work, for literature and art and heart that so benefits us all.

The Prose-Poem Project
Superstition Review
Deep Water Journal
Slipstream
Third Wednesday
Miracle Magazine
One Throne
Riverbabble
Cactus Heart
Epiphany
Your Impossible Voice
Poydras Review

Cover artwork, "Young Galaxy Accreting Material," by ESO/L. Calçada; author photo by Mary Carroll-Hackett; cover and interior book design by Diane Kistner; Book Antiqua text and titling

About FutureCycle Press

FutureCycle Press is dedicated to publishing lasting English-language poetry books, chapbooks, and anthologies in both print-on-demand and ebook formats. Founded in 2007 by long-time independent editor/publishers and partners Diane Kistner and Robert S. King, the press incorporated as a nonprofit in 2012. A number of our editors are distinguished poets and writers in their own right, and we have been actively involved in the small press movement going back to the early seventies.

The FutureCycle Poetry Book Prize and honorarium is awarded annually for the best full-length volume of poetry we publish in a calendar year. Introduced in 2013, our Good Works projects are anthologies devoted to issues of universal significance, with all proceeds donated to a related worthy cause. Our Selected Poems series highlights contemporary poets with a substantial body of work to their credit; with this series we strive to resurrect work that has had limited distribution and is now out of print.

We are dedicated to giving all of the authors we publish the care their work deserves, making our catalog of titles the most diverse and distinguished it can be, and paying forward any earnings to fund more great books.

We've learned a few things about independent publishing over the years. We've also evolved a unique, resilient publishing model that allows us to focus mainly on vetting and preserving for posterity the most books of exceptional quality without becoming overwhelmed with bookkeeping and mailing, fundraising activities, or taxing editorial and production "bubbles." To find out more about what we are doing, come see us at www.futurecycle.org.

The FutureCycle Poetry Book Prize

All full-length volumes of poetry published by FutureCycle Press in a given calendar year are considered for the annual FutureCycle Poetry Book Prize. This allows us to consider each submission on its own merits, outside of the context of a contest. Too, the judges see the finished book, which will have benefitted from the beautiful book design and strong editorial gloss we are famous for.

The book ranked the best in judging is announced as the prize-winner in the subsequent year. There is no fixed monetary award; instead, the winning poet receives an honorarium of 20% of the total net royalties from all poetry books and chapbooks the press sold online in the year the winning book was published. The winner is also accorded the honor of being on the panel of judges for the next year's competition; all judges receive copies of all contending books to keep for their personal library.

www.ingramcontent.com/pod-product-compliance
Lightning Source LLC
LaVergne TN
LVHW020939090426
835512LV00020B/3435